# PRELUDE
# TO THE
# PRESIDENCY

Recent Titles in
Contributions in Political Science
*Series Editor*: Bernard K. Johnpoll

# GARY M FINK _____

# PRELUDE TO THE PRESIDENCY

## The Political Character and Legislative Leadership Style of Governor Jimmy Carter

Contributions in Political Science, Number 40

## GREENWOOD PRESS
WESTPORT, CONNECTICUT • LONDON, ENGLAND

Grateful acknowledgment is made to the following publishers:

Jimmy Carter, *Why Not the Best?* (Nashville: Broadman Press, 1975), pp. 11, 12, 123, 124, 131, 132. All rights reserved. Used by permission.

Clinton Rossiter, *Conservatism in America: The Thankless Persuasion,* 2nd rev. ed. (New York: Alfred A. Knopf, Inc., 1962) p. 65. Copyright © Clinton Rossiter.

Library of Congress Cataloging in Publication Data

Fink, Gary M
   Prelude to the Presidency.

   (Contributions in political science; no. 40
ISSN 0147-1066)
   Bibliography: p.
   Includes index.
   1. Carter, Jimmy, 1924-   —Political career before 1976.  2. Georgia—Politics and government—1951-   3. Georgia—Executive departments—Management.  I.  Title.  II.  Series.
E873.2.F56     975.8'04'0924 [B]     79-7725
ISBN 0-313-22055-7

Library of Congress Catalog Card Number: 79-7725

ISBN: 0-313-22055-7
ISSN: 0147-1066

First published in 1980

Greenwood Press
A division of Congressional Information Service, Inc.
51 Riverside Avenue, Westport, Connecticut 06880

Printed in the United States of America

10 9 8 7 6 5 4 3 2 1

*lw*
2-10-81

*TO MY MOTHER*

MARTHA KURTZ FINK

# CONTENTS_____

viii / CONTENTS

# FIGURES

FIGURES

# TABLES

# PERSONALITY PROFILES_____

# ACKNOWLEDGMENTS_____

Numerous individuals have contributed in important ways to this endeavor. Seminar students at Georgia State University not only played a crucial role in the initiation of this project but also contributed to the development of the study. The staff at the Georgia Department of Archives and History was courteous and helpful. Several people interrupted busy schedules to discuss their experiences and perceptions with me. My indebtedness to them is increased by the failure of others to be as accommodating. The following individuals read all or parts of earlier drafts of this monograph: Senators A. W. Holloway and Hugh Carter; Richard S. Kirkendall, Indiana University; Numan V. Bartley, University of Georgia; Robert C. McMath, Georgia Institute of Technology; James W. Hilty, Temple University; Mattie S. Anderson, Emory University; and my Georgia State University colleagues, Neal C. Gillespie, James L. Maddex, Jr., and John M. Matthews. I have benefited greatly from their comments and criticisms even when, on occasion, I did not agree with them or, more commonly, simply could not answer their questions. I have also benefited from innumerable conversations on the subject with students, colleagues, friends, and acquaintances. The School of Arts and Sciences, Georgia State University, provided release time from teaching during the summer of 1978 which facilitated work on the manuscript. My wife, Mary, performed her customary and invaluable functions of sounding board, critic, editorial consultant, and proofreader. Finally, I would be remiss if I did not acknowledge the enlightened decision by Jimmy Carter to open his gubernatorial papers to public scrutiny immediately upon the conclusion of his governorship. It is to be hoped that other public officials will have the boldness to follow his example.